BIG
ISSUES

Brian Moses

Acknowledgements

Photos

Stefan May / Tony Stone Images, cover (crowd scene). Sarah Lawless / Tony Stone Images, cover (boot soles). Martin Bond / Environmental Images, page 5. Collections / Paul Watts, page 9. Sustrans / Kai / Environmental Images, page 10. Collections / Ed Gabriel, page 11. Collections / Robert Weaver, page 12 top. Stephen Whitehorne / Environmental Images, page 12 bottom. Matt Sampson / Environmental Images, page 14. Gary R. Smith / Collections, page 15. John Morrison / Environmental Images, page 16. Collections / Image Ireland / Alain Le Garsmeur, page 17. Vanessa Miles / Environmental Images, page 18. Graham Burns / Environmental Images, page 20. Hubert Raguet / Eurelios / Science Photo Library, page 24. Gontier, Jerrican / Science Photo Library, page 27.

Illustrations

Illustrations by Vali Herzer and Traffika Publishing

Heinemann Educational Publishers
Halley Court, Jordan Hill, Oxford OX2 8EJ
a division of Reed Educational & Professional Publishing Limited
www.heinemann.co.uk

Heinemann is a registered trademark of Reed Educational and Professional Publishing Limited

First published 2000
Original edition © Brian Moses, 1999
Literacy Satellites edition © Brian Moses, 2000
Additional writing for Satellites edition by Christine Butterworth

04 03 02 01
10 9 8 7 6 5 4 3 2

ISBN 0 435 11988 5   *Big Issues* single copy
ISBN 0 435 11992 3   *Big Issues* 6 copy pack

Initial design by Traffika Publishing Limited
Printed and bound in Scotland by Scotprint

Also available at Stage 4 Literacy World Satellites
ISBN 0 435 11986 9   *Alan Shearer: A Biography* single copy
ISBN 0 435 11990 7   *Alan Shearer: A Biography* 6 copy pack

ISBN 0 435 11989 3   *Quakes, Floods and Other Disasters* single copy
ISBN 0 435 11993 1   *Quakes, Floods and Other Disasters* 6 copy pack

ISBN 0 435 11987 7   *Spiders (and how they hunt)* single copy
ISBN 0 435 11991 5   *Spiders (and how they hunt)* 6 copy pack

ISBN 0 435 11995 8   *Teachers' Guide Stage 4*
ISBN 0 435 11994 X   *Guided Reading Cards Stage 4*

Contents

Introduction

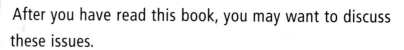

In this book there are arguments for and against four big issues: building new roads, developing the countryside, fox-hunting, and experimenting with live animals. Lots of people disagree about these issues.

After you have read this book, you may want to discuss these issues.

First, think about these points:

1 Don't speak until you are sure of what you want to say. Remember: you are trying to persuade your listeners to agree with you.

2 People will argue against you: think of what they may say, and be ready to argue back.

3 If you can, have photos, facts and figures to back up your case.

4 Listen carefully to the other side; think about their case.

5 After the discussion, think about how it went. Did you make the best case you could?

New roads

Does Havenhurst need a bypass?

Roads in Great Britain are very busy. Drivers get stressed sitting in traffic jams, and pollution from cars damages our health. But there will be even more traffic on our roads in the future, so how will we cope?

Everyone agrees that these traffic problems must be solved, but they do not agree about what the answers might be.

Some people think the answer is to build more roads, especially bypasses, which take traffic out of towns. Others say more roads spoil the countryside, and just mean more cars.

Let's look at how this argument affects Havenhurst, a large seaside town. Havenhurst's main road takes all the town's traffic along the seafront. This includes large lorries going to the ferry port. The amount of traffic is now double what it was twenty years ago.

One possible answer is to build a bypass around the town. There are arguments for and against this.

Arguments for the bypass

1 The seafront road is out of date. It was not made to carry all the traffic it gets today.

2 Driving along the seafront road is stressful for motorists, especially when there are traffic jams. A bypass would cut down on traffic jams and drivers' stress.

3 Cutting traffic on the road will mean there are fewer accidents.

4 People living by the road suffer from the noise and pollution. It is very bad for people who suffer from asthma and other breathing problems. A bypass would improve their lives.

5 Local people and visitors would get in and out of town faster using a bypass.

6 A bypass would mean better road links for the town. This would bring new shops and factories, providing local jobs.

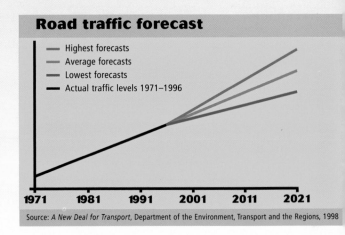

Road traffic forecast

— Highest forecasts
— Average forecasts
— Lowest forecasts
— Actual traffic levels 1971–1996

1971 1981 1991 2001 2011 2021

Source: *A New Deal for Transport*, Department of the Environment, Transport and the Regions, 1998

Graph showing how much traffic may increase. Building new roads is one way to cope with the rise.

Letter to the local paper written by a bypass supporter

Drivers back bypass

A bypass supporter gives a leaflet to a driver stuck in a jam

The local paper features the bypass story.

Dear Sir

How can anyone be against the new bypass?

For years the town has suffered from the huge rise in traffic using the Havenhurst Road. This cannot go on.

Driving along this road is a nightmare. Rush hour jams hold everyone up. The people of Havenhurst Road live with noise and traffic fumes. If they want to move, they can't sell their houses because no-one wants to live there.

The sooner the bypass is built, the better.

Mr R.Baker
29 King Street, Havenhurst

Arguments against the bypass

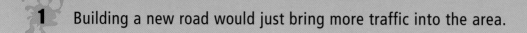

1 Building a new road would just bring more traffic into the area.

2 A bypass is not the answer. It just moves the traffic to another part of town.

3 The bypass would be built on land where rare wildlife live. Animals such as dormice might be destroyed.

4 Mostly local drivers use the Havenhurst Road. They would not use the bypass.

5 The money would be better spent on public transport. If there was a good bus service, and bus and cycle lanes, then more drivers would leave their cars at home. This would reduce traffic.

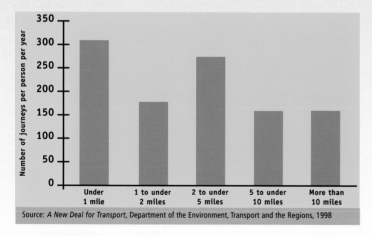

Source: *A New Deal for Transport*, Department of the Environment, Transport and the Regions, 1998

Most car journeys are very short. Getting car drivers to use other transport, not new roads, is the answer to traffic jams.

The local paper also gets letters from people against the bypass.

Dear Sir,

Last week Mr Baker wrote to your paper saying that the new bypass would cut pollution.

May I point out to Mr Baker that we can cut pollution by using our cars less, and by driving cleaner cars.

Mr Baker also says the bypass will cut traffic noise. I like to walk in the quiet country lanes where the bypass will be built. The new road will ruin the quiet countryside outside Havenhurst.

I say no to the bypass and yes to better public transport.

Mrs J.Giles
11 Roman Way, Havenhurst

Seeing both sides

Many of those who support the bypass live on the main road through Havenhurst. Heavy lorries on this road shake the foundations of their houses.

Many people think the traffic fumes can damage people's health, especially that of old people who live there. The bypass will solve their traffic problems. They also say it will be good for Havenhurst because it will bring more jobs to the town.

Other people disagree. They say the new road will not solve the problem, it will just move it to a new area. The bypass will spoil the countryside and will just bring more traffic to the area. They say the answer is better public transport - get people to use bikes on cycle tracks, or buses instead of cars.

The countryside

What sort of countryside do we want?

On a fine summer day up to 18 million people like to visit the countryside. The most popular places suffer a lot of wear and tear from crowds of visitors.

In the last twenty years, the countryside in Britain has changed a lot. New places have been built for town dwellers to visit or stay in. They visit holiday villages, garden centres, theme parks, open air museums and many other places. All this building has meant more roads and car parks that destroy the countryside.

Is it time to stop all this new development, or is it a good thing?

The next pages set out arguments for and against new development in a place called Pine Tree Valley.

Hadrian's Wall in Northumberland: thousands of people walk on it each year. This is damaging the stones.

Arguments for countryside development

1 Development can fit into the countryside. Holiday homes can be made of local wood, so they blend in with the countryside. People can do water sports on a reservoir.

2 Visitors want a choice of open-air activities, not just walking.

3 People who live in crowded cities have a right to escape to the countryside. Millions of people visit places like theme parks, so more will be needed as they become more popular.

Windsurfing on a reservoir

4 Visitors' centres can teach people how to protect the countryside.

5 These developments bring new jobs to the countryside, to replace lost farming jobs.

Wooden 'wigwams' in a holiday park blend in with the countryside.

Dear Sir,

I have read the letters your paper has printed from people who are against the new holiday village, water park and information centre proposed for Pine Tree Valley.

As the Development Manager for this scheme, I would like people to know just what the scheme offers them. It will be open to local people as well as holiday-makers. There will be water sports such as canoeing, sailing and water-skiing on the lakes, and pony-trekking around them. We hope many kinds of birds will visit the lakes, and people can come bird-watching.

The information centre will have a local studies room for schools. They will be able to visit special exhibitions, and learn about the countryside. The scheme means 500 new jobs for the area.

Don't just take my word for it - come and talk to us at the planning meeting, next Tuesday, in the village hall.

Martin Maloney
Country Park Developments Ltd.

Arguments against countryside development

1 Too many developments are spoiling the countryside. Many of them do not fit in, upset wildlife, and spoil the look of a place.

2 New developments bring in visitors and cars that overcrowd quiet country roads.

3 We should protect the countryside, not rip out more hedges for car parks.

4 Some developments disturb and destroy places where wildlife has lived for centuries. This wildlife may die out.

5 More visitors mean more pollution.

A huge visitors' car park in Dorset.

Dear Sir,

I disagree with the letter you printed from the Development Manager of the proposed development in Pine Tree Valley. Let me put the other side of the case.

The lakes Mr Maloney talks about can only be made if much of the valley is flooded. This will destroy many plants and animals that live there. I don't want water sports – I have walked this valley for years, and I want it to stay a place of peace and quiet.

We do not need information centres, either. One of these places has even popped up on the site of our local Civil War battlefield. They are out of place, and are only good for people who are too lazy to find out information for themselves.

Stop this development.

Dr.Richard Parker (Retired)

A stone cross marking the battle site at Flodden Field in Northumberland.

Seeing both sides

On one hand, there is a view that the growing numbers of people who live in towns should be able to enjoy the countryside. People have more spare time these days, and they need a wider choice of activities to enjoy. There are still empty parts of the countryside for those who want them, but what is needed is choice for the visitors.

On the other hand, once the countryside is changed, it is changed forever. The firms in charge of development do not want it for the good of the countryside. They just want to make money. They do not care about more traffic ruining the peace and quiet.

Fox-hunting

The sport of kings?

Hunting wild animals with dogs began a thousand years ago when Norman kings hunted deer, wolves and boar.

Fox-hunting only became popular about two hundred years ago. About 215,500 people now hunt.

There are 180 packs of hounds in Britain, and they kill about 16,000 foxes each year.

The Countryside Alliance is a group which says that foxes are pests that kill thousands of farm animals. They say hunting is needed to keep the number of foxes down.

Anti-hunt groups say hunting is cruel. Most people seem to agree. In a survey, 73% of people who were asked said they wanted fox-hunting banned. The RSPCA* has called for a ban on hunting with dogs.

Here are some arguments for and against fox-hunting to help you make up your own mind.

*Royal Society for the Prevention of Cruelty to Animals.

Arguments for fox-hunting

1. The fox is a serious pest that kills about 2% of all lambs. This costs each sheep farmer about £1000 a year. 96% of sheep farmers believe that the lambs are killed by foxes that live on their farms.

2. If hunting was banned, foxes would increase. This would upset the balance of wildlife.

3. Shooting or catching foxes in traps is more cruel than hunting. These can mean slow death: a dog kills quickly with one bite to the neck.

4. Hunting helps to protect the countryside. Many hunts plant woods to give foxes cover, look after hedges and keep riding tracks open.

5. If hunting was banned, 16,000 people would lose their jobs.

'People who are against hunting don't see how much good it does to the countryside.'

Robin Page,

Countryside Restoration Trust

(*Horse and Hound Magazine*)

'People see a photo of a frightened fox, feel sorry for it, and say, 'Ban hunting'. They don't see that without hunting, more foxes would just be trapped or gassed.'

James Barrington, former leader of the League Against Cruel Sports

(*Sunday Telegraph*)

'...it is fair to say that wild animals can suffer fear for a short time. But there is no reason to think that their fear is as great or long-lasting as a human's would be.'

Scott Henderson Report on Cruelty to Wild Animals

'To farmers the fox is a vicious killer.'

Farmers' Union of Wales

(*BBC Wildlife* Magazine)

What people have said in support of hunting

Arguments against fox-hunting

1 Foxes are not such huge killers. They eat mostly rabbits, rats or dead animals, and the lambs they take are already dead, or weak. They are unlikely to live anyway. More lambs die from cold or disease than are taken by foxes.

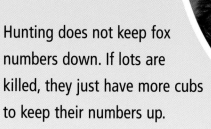

2 Hunting does not keep fox numbers down. If lots are killed, they just have more cubs to keep their numbers up.

3 Deer suffer stress when they are hunted, so foxes may too. Vets know that a bite on the neck does not kill a fox quickly.

4 There is no strong link between fox-hunting and conservation. Few landowners plant woods just for foxes.

5 The number of jobs that depend on fox-hunting is really only 1000, not the 16,000 claimed.

'The unspeakable in pursuit of the uneatable.'

Oscar Wilde, poet, dramatist and novelist

'The fact that lambs are found at foxes' earths is no evidence that they were, in fact, killed by a fox. The fox has the habit of collecting dead lambs to eat later.'

B. Vesey-Fitzgerald

(*Town Fox, Country Fox*)

'Scientific evidence shows that the fox cannot be called a pest ... in any case, hunting has little effect on fox numbers.'

Tony Soper, BBC Natural History Unit,

'In my view there is nothing more disgusting than humans killing animals for pleasure ... end blood sports.'

Eric Heffer MP

quoted in *'The Hunt and the Anti-hunt'* by P. Windeatt,

What people have said against fox-hunting

Seeing both sides

Those who support hunting say it helps to keep the numbers of foxes down. They say foxes kill lambs, and cost farmers lots of money.

Hunt supporters say hunting is not cruel, because the fox is killed very quickly. They say people who are against hunting simply do not know what goes on at a hunt.

People against hunting say that foxes are not bad for the countryside. They do an important job by killing pests, like rats and rabbits.

These critics say foxes do not always die quickly, and people should not kill a wild animal for pleasure.

The Red Fox
Friend or Foe?

What the Experts Say

League Against Cruel Sports

A leaflet from a group against fox-hunting

Vivisection

Is it right to experiment on animals?

Experimenting on living animals is called vivisection. Every year scientists use 3.5 million animals in experiments.

They mostly use rats and mice, but sometimes cats, dogs, monkeys and other small animals are used. Many animals die in these experiments.

Most of the experiments are testing drugs to cure diseases. Sometimes the animal is given a disease, or used in an operation.

People do not agree about whether it is right to use animals in this medical work. One point of view is that animals' lives are not as important as human lives. So people think this makes it right to use animals in the search for better health care for humans.

Those against vivisection say that animals have equal rights with humans and that humans are selfish to hurt animals in this work. They say that scientists have used animals for years, and have still not found a cure for diseases like cancer or AIDS.

The next pages look at the arguments for and against vivisection.

Arguments for vivisection

1. Scientists have to test new drugs on animals. Diseases such as smallpox and polio killed many people in the past. By testing medicines on animals, these diseases are now under control.

2. Scientists can find out what effect drugs have if they test them on animals. They then find out how best to use the drugs on humans.

3. Scientists learn how to do operations such as transplants by trying them out on animals first.

4. Scientists do care about the animals they use in tests. There are strict rules about how they must look after them, and they are not allowed to cause animals distress unless it will be of real use to human health.

5. Sometimes computers and test-tube experiments can replace animal experiments. But doctors still need to test medicines on animals to be sure it is safe to test them on humans.

This rat is part of an experiment to find a cure for humans with sleep problems.

Medical discoveries

Experiments on animals helped scientists develop the following:

1 Vaccines that protect against serious diseases such as polio, measles, and tetanus in humans, distemper in dogs and cat flu

2 Drugs that help people with asthma, diabetes and epilepsy to live a normal life

3 Cures for diseases that were once fatal, such as childhood leukemia

4 Modern medicines that make operations safe

These are some of the major medical discoveries of the twentieth century.

Animal experiments helped in all of them.

Animal care

Scientists care for their experimental animals. These are the '3Rs': basic rules of good animal care.

1 Replace the use of animals whenever possible.

2 Refine tests so they hurt the animals as little as possible.

3 Reduce the use of animals needed (to the smallest number possible).

1920s Insulin, for diabetics
1930s drugs to block pain
1940s Penicillin
1950s Polio vaccine, kidney transplants
1960s transplants to restore sight
1970s drugs for asthma and ulcers
1980s life support systems for premature babies
1990s vaccine for meningitis

Arguments against vivisection

1. Scientists do not need to keep looking for new drugs and using animals. People's living conditions have been getting better, and this has led to a fall in diseases.

2. Animals do not always react to drugs like humans, so some test results can be wrong.

3. People would not need so many drugs if they lived a healthier lifestyle, for example, if they stopped smoking, and stopped drinking too much. This would cut the number of animal experiments needed to test drugs.

4. Even with rules, these animals are still made to suffer. Experiments are often done without giving the animals painkillers, and they must live in cages.

5. Scientists should look harder for other ways to do their experiments.

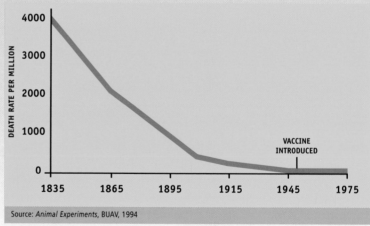

Source: *Animal Experiments*, BUAV, 1994

This graph shows deaths from tuberculosis in England and Wales between 1835 and 1975. The line shows how deaths were falling, even before the vaccine, because people's lives were healthier.

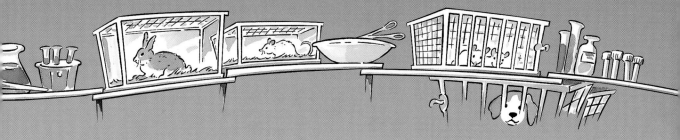

Can we trust results?

Do animal experiments give true results?

1 Penicillin kills guinea pigs and hamsters, so if this valuable drug had been tested on them, humans would never have got it.

2 The drug morphine calms humans – but drives cats wild.

3 Humans can take aspirin, but it damages the young of many animals, including cats and dogs.

4 Thalidomide was a drug taken by pregnant women. It was tested safely on rats and mice, but caused terrible damage to human babies: some were born without arms or legs.

5 Eraldin was a heart drug that did not harm animals. It caused serious damage, even blindness, in humans.

6 Opren was a drug that cured arthritis in rats, but when humans took it, over 3500 reported damage. Over 60 people died in Britain.(from *Animal Kind, Early Times*)

Monkeys like to live in large groups. They can suffer great stress when they are kept alone for testing.

Seeing both sides

Animal experiments have led to many discoveries that help humans, such as heart and kidney transplants. People with conditions such as asthma and epilepsy can lead normal lives. These benefits lead many people to say that vivisection should go on because it helps prevent human suffering and death.

On the other hand, the results of animal tests are not always the same with humans. Drugs that have been tested have later caused damage to humans. Thousands of animals are made to suffer for no good purpose.

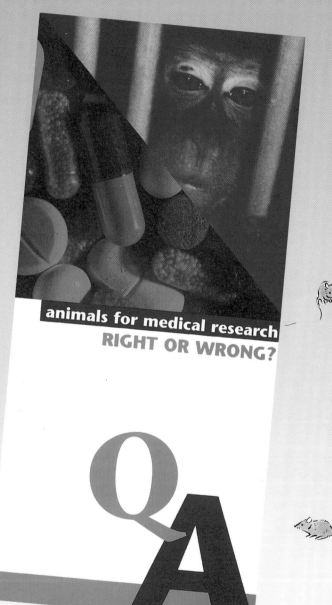

animals for medical research
RIGHT OR WRONG?

A leaflet from the British Union for the Abolition of Vivisection (BUAV).

How can you get your views across?

This book has shown you different ways to put across an argument. If you want to have your views heard, make sure you know your facts. On page 31 there is a list of organisations that will send out information on different issues. You can write to 'The Publicity Officer' in each one. Begin your letter, 'Dear Sir/Madam'.

You may want to write to your favourite magazine about one of the issues here. If the issue is a local one, try writing to the local paper. Address your letter to the Editor.

Ask for views around your school. Who agrees with you? What do they want to do about it?

You could display your views for others to see. You may be able to put eye-catching posters on a notice-board or wall.

Try to think up a catchy slogan for your issue. Make it easy to remember. Use rhyme, or puns, as they do in adverts.

What about presenting a school assembly on your issue? You can use posters, poems or plays, or present the assembly as a radio or TV broadcast.

Would your local radio station let you air your views? Write and ask them.

Once you get started, you will probably get more ideas to help you get your message across.

Good luck!

Useful addresses

New roads

Department of Transport, 2 Marsham Street, London, SW1 P 3EB

Transport 2000, Walkden House, 10 Melton Street, London, NW1 2EJ

The countryside

Council for the Protection of Rural England, 25 Buckingham Palace Road, London, SW1W 0PP

Campaign for the Countryside (same address as above)

Fox-hunting

Countryside Alliance, The Old Town Hall, 367 Kennington Road, London, SE11 4PT

League Against Cruel Sports, 83–87 Union Street, London, SE1 1SG

RSPCA, Causeway, Horsham, West Sussex, RH12 1HG

The International Fund for Animal Welfare, Warren Court, Park Road, Crowborough, East Sussex, TN6 2GA

Vivisection

Seriously Ill for Medical Research, P.O. Box 504, Dunstable, Bedfordshire, LU6 2LU

Animals in Medicines Research Information Centre, 12 Whitehall, London, SW1A 2DY

British Union for the Abolition of Vivisection, 16a Crane Grove, London, N7 8LB

National Anti-Vivisection Society, 261 Goldhawk Road, London, W12 9PE

Bibliography

Barton, Miles, *Animal Rights* (Franklin Watts, 1989)

Bright, M., *Traffic Pollution* (Franklin Watts, 1991)

Bronze, Lewis; Heathcote, Nick; and Brown, Peter, *The Blue Peter Green Book* (BBC Books / Sainsbury's, 1990)

James, Barbara, *Animal Rights* (Wayland, 1990)

Moses, Brian, *Somewhere to Be – Language and the Environment* (A resource book for teachers at KS2) (WWF, 1992)

The organisations in the 'Useful addresses' section above also produce useful leaflets and other publications about the issues discussed in this book.

Index